MUD HOUSE

By Rowena Mouda
Illustrated by Kara Matters

Library For All Ltd.

Library For All is an Australian not for profit organisation with a mission to make knowledge accessible to all via an innovative digital library solution. Visit us at libraryforall.org

Mud House

First published 2023

Published by Library For All Ltd
Email: info@libraryforall.org
URL: libraryforall.org

Our Yarning logo design by Jason Lee, Bidjipidji Art

Original illustrations by Kara Matters

Mud House
Mouda, Rowena
ISBN: 978-1-922991-12-6
SKU03392

MUD HOUSE

We respect and honour Aboriginal and Torres Strait Islander Elders past, present and future. We acknowledge the stories, traditions and living cultures of Aboriginal and Torres Strait Islander peoples on this land and commit to building a brighter future together.

One afternoon in Derby, two boys, Lanty and Le'zak, go to the marsh near their home.

Lanty says, "Let's make
a mud house."

The two boys start smashing
the mud to make the house.

Le'zak says, "We need water," and gets some from the big puddle nearby.

The boys mix the mud and water, which turns into clay.

Together, they start to plan
and build the mud house.

The mud is gooey and squishy
on their hands and feet.

As the sun sets on the marsh,
Lanty and Le'zak finish making
their mud house.

They are pleased with
their work.

The boys laugh and smile as they run home to their family and tell them about their mud house on the marsh.

You can use these questions to talk about this book with your family, friends and teachers.

What did you learn from this book?

Describe this book in one word. Funny? Scary? Colourful? Interesting?

How did this book make you feel when you finished reading it?

What was your favourite part of this book?

About the contributors

Rowena was born in Derby, Western Australia, from the Dari, Oomeday, Yowjabai and Nyikina groups. She loves sharing stories, fishing and being with family. Rowena's favourite stories are her grandmother's family stories about when she was young.

Kara is a Noongar artist from Albany, Western Australia, with extensive experience in acrylic painting, digital art, illustration and design. Inspiration comes to Kara in all forms; she draws from the Earth, the Ocean, and what connects her emotionally to Country and soul.

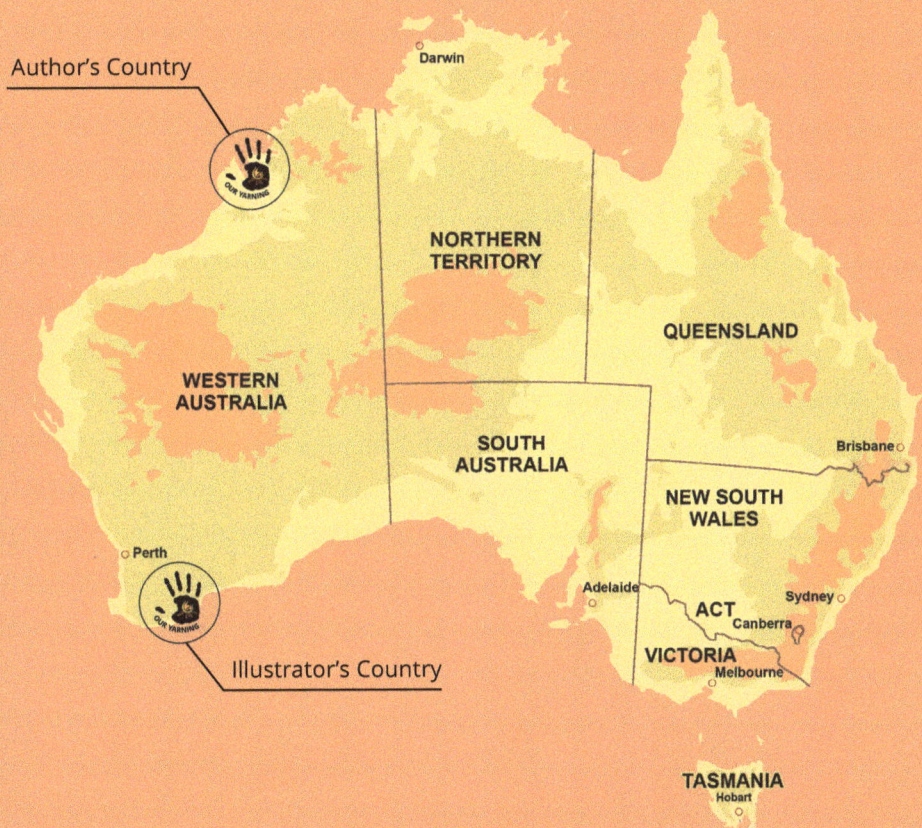

Author's Country

Darwin

NORTHERN TERRITORY

QUEENSLAND

WESTERN AUSTRALIA

SOUTH AUSTRALIA

Brisbane

NEW SOUTH WALES

Perth

Adelaide

Sydney

ACT
Canberra

Illustrator's Country

VICTORIA
Melbourne

TASMANIA
Hobart

Our Yarning

Want to discover more books from this collection? Our Yarning is a collection of books written by Aboriginal and Torres Strait Islander peoples across Australia.

We know that children learn better, and enjoy reading more, when they see themselves in the stories, characters and illustrations of the books they read.

To download the app, visit the Google Play Store on any Android device and search 'Our Yarning'.

libraryforall.org